Explore
Music
through
Stories

David Wheway and
Shelagh Thomson

16 varied national curriculum
Music activities linked to the
English attainment targets

Music Department
OXFORD UNIVERSITY PRESS
Oxford and New York

Oxford University Press, Walton Street, Oxford OX2 6DP, England

Oxford is a trade mark of Oxford University Press

First published 1993
ISBN 0 19 321868 2
Design and illustration by Creative Intelligence, Bristol
Printed in Great Britain by Caligraving Ltd., Thetford, Norfolk

Acknowledgements
The Mouse and the Doves and *The Buddha and the Elephant* from *Multi Faith Fables* © Mary Glasgow Publications Ltd., London

Pan Gu by Shiu Yuan-ming and Stuart Thompson from *Chinese Stories* © 1986 Wayland (Publishers) Ltd.

Contents

There are nine books in this series:

Explore Music through

> Art, Geography, History, Maths, Movement,
> Poetry and Rhyme, Science, Stories, Word Games.

Introduction

These booklets are designed for primary teachers who value the role of music in an integrated approach to the curriculum. They are of equal value to those who have little or no experience of teaching music, or those who have responsibility as a music co-ordinator.

By closely relating musical activities to other areas of the curriculum, it is hoped that primary teachers will feel more confident when engaging in musical activities with children.

Within each of the nine booklets in the series, activities are ordered progressively from 'early years' through to upper Key Stage 2.

The appropriateness of any activity will depend on the previous experience of the child or group. For this reason we have not recommended any activity for a specific age group, but have indicated a target Key Stage.

Many activities, especially those primarily concerned with composition, are often best delivered over a number of sessions. This allows time for exploratory work, and also for evaluation, discussion, and development.

Building a Repertoire of Sounds

Children need an ever-increasing knowledge of sounds, and teachers need to be aware of the importance of sound exploration for future musical activities. This repertoire of sounds is especially important when children wish to represent feelings, objects, and other sounds in their compositions.

Body and Vocal Sounds

Children should explore the possibility for sounds made both vocally and with the body. For instance, how many sounds can be made with the throat? ('Ooooh', 'Ahhhh', a hiccup, a cough, a gargle, humming, sighing, panting, etc.) What different sounds can be made by patting different parts of the body? (Cheeks, chest, stomach, thighs, knees, etc.)

Classroom Percussion

Children should be encouraged to find as many different ways as possible to play percussion. Can it be scraped, tapped, shaken, scratched, blown, etc.? When a new sound is found, think about what moods or images it conjures up. Such exploration works well in small groups, using a limited number of instruments. Allow the children time to play new sounds to the rest of the class.

Percussion Resources

Some considerations when building resources:

Do your percussion resources offer a wide choice for creating a variety of sounds?

Are the instruments made from a variety of materials (e.g. wood, metal, plastic, etc.)?

Does the collection contain instruments from different ethnic origins?

Are the instruments of good quality? Remember, as in other areas of the curriculum, poor quality materials (e.g. worn or broken) may lead to poor or disappointing results.

Other Sound Makers

A wide variety of sounds can be made with everyday objects such as paper, kitchen utensils, beads and pulses (e.g. paper tearing, scrunching, flapping; pulses poured into a bucket, swirled around, shaken; pots and pans drum-kit).

When performing any activity, try different combinations of sound, as this adds to the children's exploratory work, and their understanding of timbre and texture.

Recording

It is very important that children develop ways of recording their compositions. A variety of ways are suggested throughout the booklets, for example, pictures, symbols, words, letters, and so on. Ensure paper and appropriate recording materials are always available.

Audio as well as video recorders are also valuable resources for recording children's work and development.

The Activities

Suggested Materials

These materials should be useful as a guide for preparing the lessons. They are only suggestions and teachers may wish to select their own materials.

Suggested Listening

Generally, it is a good idea to keep extracts short, e.g. 30–60 seconds in duration. If possible, tape-record extracts beforehand to avoid searching in the lesson.

Most of the suggestions given are easily available in record libraries or through record shops. Many can be found on compilations. Where this is not the case, a reference is given.

The recordings we have recommended should not be considered either obligatory or comprehensive.

Personal collections of recorded music are a valuable resource. However, do avoid limiting the children's listening opportunities to any one type of music.

Attainment Target Boxes

The left-hand box gives an indication of the main focus of each activity, relating to the national curriculum for Music. However it should be noted that the activities will also offer a variety of other musical experiences.

The right-hand box indicates how the activity may complement work undertaken in another area of the curriculum.

Classroom Organization

For many whole-class activities, a circle of children on a carpet or chairs is ideal. This helps concentration and promotes a feeling of involvement, as well as being practical when it comes to observing other children, whole-group involvement, and passing games. It might be advisable at times to split the class or set into groups.

There are some activities that require little or no percussion, and if you are just starting out you may feel more confident attempting these activities initially.

Handing Out Instruments

Avoid the children making a headlong rush to the music trolley at all costs! Allow the children to collect, or hand out, a few instruments at a time.

– Have the required instruments placed out ready beforehand.
– While listening to instructions, children should place their instruments on the floor in front of them.
– Give out beaters for instruments last.

- Before commencing agree on clear signals for stopping and putting instruments down (e.g. a hand in the air, a finger to the lips, a wink of the eye, etc.).
- Demand an immediate response to these signals.
- Encourage children to treat instruments with respect at all times. (This is not easy if instruments are worn or broken.)

Evaluation and Appraisal

When children are working on a composition, there should be regular evaluation by the teacher, and/or by the children, of how the work is progressing. This will include a great deal of purposeful listening and appraising. The process will in turn help the children in appraising the music of others.

Key Questions for Performers and Audience

Can you tell us about your music?

How did the piece start/finish?

What did you like about it?

What contrasts/changes did the piece contain?

Does the piece fulfil the task set?

Was it performed fluently and appropriately?

Could it have been improved, and if so, how?

Could the piece be extended, and if so, how? (e.g. repetition, contrasts, new material, different instruments, etc.)

Did the audience listen well?

Peace at Last

Suggested Materials

Book: *Peace at Last* by Jill Murphy, published by Macmillan. A variety of percussion, and other sound makers.

1. Many short stories for young children lend themselves to the addition of sound effects. A particularly good example is *Peace at Last* by Jill Murphy. The ideas opposite are suggestions only. Children should be encouraged to put forward their own ideas.

2. When the story is first told to the children, discuss with them which parts of the story could have a 'sound effect', and what sound would be appropriate.

3. Tell the story through again, and pause to allow the chosen sound to be made.

4. As the children become familiar with the story, encourage them to anticipate the occasion when the sound effect is appropriate and to join in of their own accord.

Music Attainment Target: 1 & 2 Main Focus: Exploring Sounds Key Stage: 1	English Attainment Target: 1 Main Focus: Story

Suggestions for sounds:

Going to bed	– xylophone played from bottom to top
Snoring	– guiro scraped, yoghurt pot filled with rice, vocal snoring sounds
Walking	– claves, fingers on a table
Aeroplane	– vocal engine sounds
Clock	– two-tone woodblock, two pencils tapped together
Walking	– as before
Water	– chime bars, milk bottle organ (bottles filled with differing levels of water)
Fridge	– maracas, vocal hum
Walking	– as before
Owl	– mouthpiece of recorder, vocal owl hoot
Hedgehog	– tambour or piece of paper lightly scraped with fingernails
Cats	– vocal 'miaow'
Walking	– as before
Birds	– bells shaken, triangle played quickly
Sun	– cymbal played lightly, yoghurt pot filled with sand and moved appropriately
Walking	– as before
Alarm bell	– bells, whole class vocal 'drrriiing' as a finale!

There are lots of stories that can be added to in this way. Not only does it add to the enjoyment of the story, but it offers the children valuable experience in the exploration and evaluation of sounds within a context.

The Enormous Turnip

Suggested Materials

Access to a variety of percussion. Story: *The Great Big Enormous Turnip* by Alexei Tolstoy.

1. This story is one which is very repetitive and cumulative, and therefore ideal to use as a framework to develop sequencing of sound.

2. Read the story to the children and make a list of the characters.

3. With the children choose different sounds to represent each character, e.g.

> **Old Man** – bass xylophone
> **Old Woman** – alto xylophone
> **Granddaughter** – glockenspiel
> **Black Dog** – woodblock
> **Cat** – tambourine
> **Mouse** – triangle.

4. Read the story again, each instrument being played when its character is mentioned.

Music Attainment Target: 1 & 2 Main Focus: Composing and Form Key Stage: 1	English Attainment Target: 1 & 2 Main Focus: Story Structure

Storying from Sound

Suggested Materials

One piece of percussion or sound maker per child.

1. The children sit in a circle, with a sound maker in front of them. Each child plays their instrument in turn. The teacher asks the children to decide what each sound makes them think of, e.g. 'water', 'thunder', 'someone chattering', 'the wind', etc.

   The teacher writes down each sound and suggestion.

2. The results should then be categorized, e.g. all water sounds, animal sounds, etc.

3. The teacher then creates a short story or situation from these sounds, e.g. 'The bear woke up and walked down to the river. It started to rain . . . '

   The children make their sounds at the appropriate time.

Extension Activities

Children might like to go on to doing their own 'storying' from sounds, in small groups or as a whole-class activity.

Music Attainment Target: 1 & 2	English Attainment Target: 1
Main Focus: Exploring Sounds	Main Focus: Storying
Key Stage: 1	

Goldilocks

Suggested Materials

Access to a variety of percussion and other sound makers.

1. A story trail is an excellent way of encouraging composing. The chosen story should be reduced to five or six salient episodes or events. Sounds are then created to illustrate these.

2. Children could be divided into groups, to create the sounds/music for an allotted part of the story. Below is an example of how the well-known story of *Goldilocks and the Three Bears* might be adapted.

Events:

a) Goldilocks walks into the bears' house.

b) Eats porridge.

c) Breaks baby's chair.

d) Goes upstairs and falls asleep.

e) Bears return, and Goldilocks runs off.

3. Suggestions for sounds:

Body and vocal	– squelching for eating; slap legs for walking; vocal snoring and roaring.
Instrumental	– xylophone low notes to high for going upstairs; castanets, guiro and drum/cymbal crash for breaking chair; scraping tambour for spoon in bowl.
Other sound makers	– pulses shaken in yoghurt pot for walking across gravel; pots and pans for bears' return; crumpled paper for eating.

Music Attainment Target: 1 Main Focus: Exploring and Composing Key Stage: 1	English Attainment Target: 1 Main Focus: Story

The Three Little Pigs

Suggested Materials

Body/vocal sounds, percussion, and other sound makers.

1. Discuss the story with the children.

2. The story can be performed as in **Goldilocks**. With the children select sounds to use and to add to the story. The following suggestions may help:

Three little pigs running around
> – vocal squeaks, bells played quickly.

Wolf prowling around
> – drum repeated as footsteps.

First little pig builds a house of straw
> – rubbing palms, finger stroking drumskin, scrunching raffia or paper.

Wolf tries to blow first pig's house down, and succeeds
> – three vocal puffs, wolf footsteps continue, cymbal crash for house falling, bells for pig running away.

Second little pig builds a house of sticks
> – maracas for sawing, rhythm sticks, claves.

Wolf tries to blow second pig's house down, and succeeds
> – repeat as for straw house.

Third little pig builds a house of bricks
> – tap woodblocks together.

Wolf tries to blow third pig's house down, but fails
> – vocal puffs followed by panting.

Wolf climbs up the house and then falls down the chimney
> – ascending notes on tuned percussion, followed by cymbal crash and bang on drum. Vocal cheers.

Music Attainment Target: 1
Main Focus: Exploring and Composing
Key Stage: 1

English Attainment Target: 1
Main Focus: Traditional Story

Jack and the Beanstalk

Suggested Materials

Access to a variety of percussion.

This well-known story is easily adapted to use as a story trail.

1. **Events:**
   a) Jack takes the cow to market and exchanges the cow for beans.
   b) The beans grow into a giant creeper and Jack climbs up and finds a castle.
   c) Jack hides in the castle and hears the giant.
   d) The giant counts his money and then falls asleep. Jack runs off with the money and climbs back down the beanstalk.
   e) When the gold has been spent Jack climbs back up the beanstalk.
   f) Jack hides in the castle and sees the giant with a hen that lays golden eggs.
   g) After the giant has fallen asleep Jack snatches the hen and climbs back down the beanstalk.
   h) After a while Jack grows restless and decides to climb back up the beanstalk and visit the castle once again.
   i) The giant is listening to a harp that plays beautiful music on command.
   j) As before, Jack waits for the giant to fall asleep and then he creeps out and steals the harp.
   k) Suddenly the giant wakes up and chases Jack.
   l) Quickly Jack climbs down the beanstalk and chops it down.

Music Attainment Target: 1 Main Focus: Composing Key Stage: 1	English Attainment Target: 1 Main Focus: Story

2. Suggestions for sound:

    a) Coconut shells and claves for Jack and the cow walking to market.

    b) Pitched percussion played from low to high for the beanstalk growing. Claves for Jack climbing.

    c) Slow, heavy drumbeat for giant. Children chant:

> *Fee Fi Fo Fum*
> *I smell the blood of an Englishman*
> *Be he alive, or be he dead*
> *I'll grind his bones to make my bread.*

    d) Bells jingle for money, guiro for snoring. Claves played quickly for Jack running.

    e) Pitched percussion played high to low, with footsteps on claves, for Jack climbing down.

    f) Vocal sounds for hen squawking.

    g) Gentle flowing sequence on tuned percussion for harp.

    h) Drum roll and cymbal crash for beanstalk falling down.

Extension Activities

Try performing without words, letting the sounds tell the story. The resulting music could be used to accompany a short piece of drama based on the story of Jack and the Beanstalk. You may like to have a picture of the beanstalk next to a xylophone. Can the children play some 'beanstalk growing' music? (Encourage the children to play the xylophone using a beater in each hand.)

Walter the Worm

Suggested Materials

An assortment of paper.

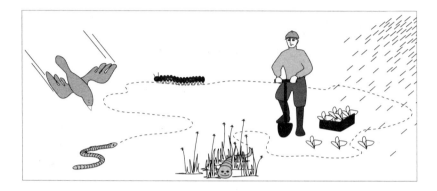

1. Find sounds using paper to illustrate the stages in the above picture story, e.g.

   - slithering worm (slide hands over paper)
   - bird attacks (wave sheets of paper in air)
   - meets centipede (hold edges of sheets of paper and tug lightly and rhythmically)
   - man digging (hold sheet of paper in air and slap)
   - rain (lightly drum tips of fingers on paper held in air)
   - moving through the grass (scrunch paper)

2. Now perform the trail with children playing in the appropriate places. It may be helpful if you follow the trail with your finger or a pointer.

Extension Activities

Repeat this activity using a variety of percussion instruments.

Music Attainment Target: 1 Main Focus: Composing Key Stage: 1	English Attainment Target: 1 Main Focus: Storying

Character Motifs

Suggested Materials

Access to a variety of tuned and untuned percussion.

Suggested Listening

Extracts from *Peter and the Wolf* by Prokofiev, *Carnival of the Animals* by Saint-Saëns, *Nutcracker Suite* by Tchaikovsky.

1. Extend the ideas in **'The Enormous Turnip'**, by representing each character with a theme 'motif'. (An example of this idea for children to listen to is *Peter and the Wolf* by Prokofiev.)

2. Using the story of **'The Enormous Turnip'** (or one with a similar cumulative structure), ask the children to represent the characters not with one sound alone, but with a sequence. This could be a short melody or rhythm, e.g.

   Old Man – low, slow tune on a bass xylophone, with slow drumbeat.
   Old Woman – slow tune, on medium-pitched notes.
   Granddaughter – fast, high tune on a glockenspiel.
   Black Dog – a short rhythmic pattern repeated four times.
   Cat – four shakes on a tambourine followed by a vocal miaow.
   Mouse – bells shaken followed by a triangle played three times.

3. Practise each 'motif' so it can be repeated accurately each time.

4. Incorporate the 'motifs' into a narration of the story.

Extension Activities

Can the children find ways of recording their sounds on paper? This might be through the use of letters, numbers, symbols etc. Remember there are no 'right' or 'wrong' solutions.

Music Attainment Target: 1 & 2 Main Focus: Composing Motifs Key Stage: 1/2	English Attainment Target: 1 & 2 Main Focus: Characterization

The Mouse and the Doves

Suggested Materials

Cards with pictures on e.g.

The story:

One day, while a flock of white doves were looking for food, they saw a little mouse nibbling seeds below them. The Dove-King noticed a fierce hawk just about to swoop down on the mouse. The hawk spread its wings and began its attack, when all at once the doves flew between the hawk and its prey. This slowed the hawk down and the mouse scampered to safety.

The hungry doves flew on and saw some rice under a tree. The doves glided down and pecked on the rice. But it was a trap! A net fell down from the tree and trapped all the doves.

The doves could hear the farmer who had set the trap coming nearer and nearer. Just as the farmer got to the net the whole flock flapped together like a giant bird and managed to lift the net in their beaks and fly away. The farmer chased after them but the doves managed to fly out of his reach.

The doves were very tired and found they could not now escape from the net they were carrying. Suddenly the Dove-King remembered the mouse and led the flock back to where it had been. The mouse saw the doves, tired and hungry and struggling with the net, so it carefully released the doves by gnawing through the net with its good sharp teeth.

The mouse and the doves had helped and protected each other and would be friends for the rest of their lives.

1. Read the story to the children and discuss appropriate sounds for the different characters, e.g.

   Doves – soft, gentle, flowing sounds (glissandos on glockenspiels, vocal cooing, bells played lightly);

   Mouse – fast, high, scampering (maracas, high chime bars played quickly, vocal squeaks);

   Hawk – loud, sudden, angry (guiros scraped hard, cymbals crashed, vibraslap);

   Farmer – footsteps (drums, claves).

2. Divide the children into four groups, one for each character. Display the cards showing the pictures of the characters. Listen to each group (they should only play when you are pointing to their picture), and discuss the performances. Can they be improved in any way? (e.g. was the dove music soft enough? Did the hawk music sound angry? etc.).

3. Perform, with you narrating the story. Control the music by pointing to the picture cards.

Music Attainment Target: 1 & 2
Main Focus: Composing
Key Stage: 1/2

English Attainment Target: 1
Main Focus: Story

The Wind and the Sun

Suggested Materials

Access to a variety of percussion.

The story:

The wind and the sun are having an argument to see who is the stronger. After a while they see a man walking along. 'Look here,' says the wind, 'I am so strong, I bet I could blow that man's coat off.'

The wind and sun agree that whichever of them can remove the coat from the man is the stronger.

The wind starts to blow, and the man, noticing the sudden chill in the air, pulls his coat tightly around him. The wind blows harder, so the man fastens all the buttons on his coat, and ties the strap. So the wind blows even harder. But the harder the wind blows, the tighter the man holds on to his coat. Very soon the wind is exhausted and gives up.

'Now it's my turn,' says the sun.

'Ha, what chance do you stand,' pants the wind. 'You can't blow at all!'

But the sun merely smiles, and begins to glow. The man, noticing the warmth, undoes his coat. The sun glows warmer, and the man begins to mop his brow. It is soon too hot to be wearing his heavy coat, and so he takes it off and carries it over his arm. The sun has won the bet.

1. With the children, explore possible sounds for the wind. These could be vocal sounds, swirling sounds on maracas and other shakers, newspaper sheets waved in the air, rubbing legs, rubbing the skins of tambours and drums. Experiment with getting louder and quieter.

2. Discuss what sounds could be used for the sun, e.g. chime bars entering one by one as the sun grows hotter; large cymbals becoming louder and quieter; vocal humming.

3. Use these sounds to accompany the narration of the story.

Extension Activities

Can the children think of symbols to represent the sounds of the wind and the sun? e.g.

  or

The children could use these symbols to make sound sequences, e.g.

They may choose to play sounds together, e.g.

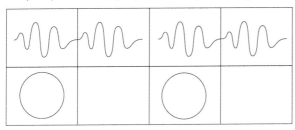

The children may like to add other weather sounds and symbols (e.g. for rain).

Music Attainment Target: 1 & 2	English Attainment Target: 1 & 2
Main Focus: Composing	Main Focus: Traditional Story
Key Stage: 1/2	

The Tortoise and the Hare

Suggested Materials

Access to a variety of percussion.

This well-known fable can be easily adapted for use as a story trail. The following suggestions may help:

1. **Events**

   a) The hare and the tortoise begin the race. Children chant, 'Ready, steady, go' followed by fast 'footsteps' on claves (hare) and very slow footsteps on a tambour (tortoise).

   b) The hare stops under a tree and falls asleep. The tortoise plods on! Tambour continues as above. Claves stop, replaced by vocal snores.

   c) The hare wakes up and sees the tortoise nearly at the finishing line so he quickly sprints for the finish. Tambour continues. Claves join in, playing very quickly.

   d) The tortoise wins and everyone celebrates. Tambour and claves gradually slow down. Vocal cheers.

   (Involve the whole class in the performance by using patting knees for the tambour and two fingers on the palm of a hand for the claves.)

2. Tell the story to the children, or let one of them tell it, while two children mime the story, matching their movements to the sounds.

Extension Activities

1. Having performed with the teacher narrating the story, try performing with the music only; the children will need to listen to each other carefully for cues.

2. Discuss with the children the difference in pace when playing the sound for the hare, and the sound for the tortoise. The hare has a fast pace, the tortoise a slow pace.

   Children may like to work from a chart such as the one suggested below, or make their own using different elements of pace.

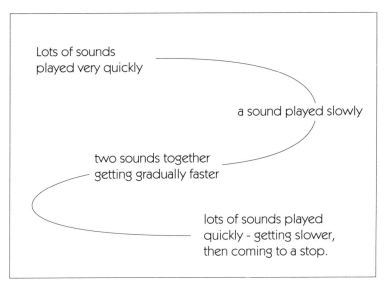

Lots of sounds played very quickly

a sound played slowly

two sounds together getting gradually faster

lots of sounds played quickly - getting slower, then coming to a stop.

Music Attainment Target: 1 & 2 Main Focus: Composing and Pace Key Stage: 2	English Attainment Target: 1 & 2 Main Focus: Fable

The Iron Man

Suggested Materials

A copy of the book *The Iron Man* by Ted Hughes, published by Faber and Faber. Collection of metal objects (see below).

The idea for this activity is related to the story *The Iron Man*, by Ted Hughes, but relates equally to any work on moving mechanical objects.

1. Ask the children to bring in as many metal objects as they can. (Obviously warn them about dangerous things such as knives, tin can lids, etc.)

2. Once the objects have been collected, allow the children time to experiment, possibly in groups, to see how many different sounds they can get from their metal objects. Can they be tapped? Do different beaters create different effects? Can they be brushed or scraped? What sounds can be achieved by pouring counters, pulses, sand, etc. into pots, pans, tins . . . ?

3. Can the children, in groups, now compose a short piece of music using their metal instruments and the story as a stimulus? Ask them to make a list of sounds they wish to represent, e.g. the man walking, eating, falling over the cliff, lying on a fire, etc.

Encourage the children to structure their music carefully, thinking of the following:

How will the piece start?
How will the piece finish?
What contrasts/changes will the piece contain?

Music Attainment Target: 1 & 2 Main Focus: Exploring and Composing Key Stage: 2	English Attainment Target: 1 & 2 Main Focus: Story

Children's Stories

Suggested Materials

Children's own stories. Variety of percussion.

1. Children's own stories often lend themselves to 'story trails'. To decide if
   a child's story offers the opportunity for a trail, consider the following:

   Are there adjectives within the story that describe sound?
   Are there characters within the story that can have their own sound or
   theme?
   What opportunities are there for atmospheric sounds?

The Haunted House

Suddenly we woke up – something had disturbed
us – what was that sound? We crept quietly
out of the room – what were all the creaks
and groans ?...

2. The children may like to produce a picture score from their stories. This
   could be used as an aid to performance.

Music Attainment Target: 1
Main Focus: Composing
Key Stage: 2

English Attainment Target: 3
Main Focus: Story Writing

The Story of Pan Gu

Suggested Materials

Access to a variety of percussion.

This ancient Chinese story tells of how the world began. It is full of strong images and therefore can be used effectively as a stimulus for music composition. The story can be divided into six parts, enabling groups of children to work on each part before combining together to form a class piece. The story is reproduced below, together with some suggestions to start the children off.

1. In the beginning was nothing. All was gloomy and dark. The universe was like a giant egg. Inside, alone, in darkness was Pan Gu, curled up in a deep sleep.

   A sequence of 'dark, gloomy' sounds; repeated slow drumbeat; vocal breathing.

2. Slowly Pan Gu woke up. He hated the darkness and he punched and kicked his shell trying to escape. Suddenly he broke out. This bursting out caused chaos outside. Light things floated up, heavy things sank. The sky had separated from the earth! Light appeared. Pan Gu could see!

   As 1, gradually becoming louder and quicker. Banging and crashing. Irregular sounds. Cymbal crash. Xylophones, and glockenspiels played from top to bottom. Shimmering tambourines and finger cymbals.

3. Pan Gu wanted the earth and the sky further apart, so they could never join again. So, for years he pushed the sky upwards with his shoulders and created a gap that could never be closed.

   Starting on middle notes, play to the top and bottom at the same time on glockenspiels and xylophones. Play loudly then gradually get quieter.

4. Pan Gu had used all his strength. He collapsed, dying. His last breaths became winds, and his dying grunts, thunder.

Staggered beats on a drum.
Wind sounds – vocal; maracas.
Thunder – drum rolls.

5. Pan Gu's body made the world more beautiful. His blood flowed and became rivers. His body made mountains, his hair made stars, his sweat made rain, and his eyes made the sun and the moon.

Glissandos on tuned percussion.
Chime bars – stars.
Triangle – rain.
Finger cymbals – moon and sun.

6. People say that Pan Gu did not really die, but stays with us in the miracles of nature around us. He is happy that he has created such a beautiful world.

Sequence from section 1 played, gradually dying out.

Music Attainment Target: 1
Main Focus: Composing
Key Stage: 2

English Attainment Target: 1 & 2
Main Focus: Chinese Story

The Buddha and the Elephant

Suggested Materials

See suggestions in chart below.

Suggested Listening

Extracts from recordings of Indian ragas.

Like the previous story, **Pan Gu**, this story offers many opportunities for composition.

1. The Buddha's cousin, Devadatta, was jealous of the Buddha and plotted to get rid of him. One day Buddha was preaching to villagers when Devadatta noticed a number of elephants nearby. They stood quietly flapping their ears against the flies, and gently swinging their trunks.

Background: low, calm, peaceful tune, played slowly throughout the section.
Sound effects: flapping ears – pieces of paper flapped; buzzing flies – maracas, cabasa.

2. Devadatta asked the elephant keeper for an elephant for the Buddha to use. Devadatta led the elephant away to a hidden yard.

Background: tune continues at the same sedate pace.
Sound effects: footsteps; elephant – drum; Devadatta – claves.

3. Devadatta sent for some rice wine and gave the elephant lots of wine to drink. The elephant loved the wine and drank through his trunk from a bucket.

Background: tune continues, gradually speeding up.
Sound effects: vocal slurping; glockenspiel played quickly from low to high for wine travelling up trunk.

4. Devadatta gave the elephant to a group of monks to give to the Buddha as a present. The monks tried to lead the elephant out of the yard but it started to stagger and grow angry. The elephant broke loose and bellowed loudly.

Background: tune continues at faster pace.
Sound effects: elephant's staggering footsteps – drum; bellowing – cymbal and guiro.

5. The Buddha heard a terrible noise, getting louder and louder. There were screams and crashes as the elephant rampaged through the village. The Buddha looked into the elephant's mind and knew why the animal was behaving like this.

Background: tune very fast, played wildly.
Sound effects: vocal screams, cymbal crashes, drum rolls; footsteps and bellowing as for section 4.

6. The Buddha faced the elephant as it came charging noisily towards him. All the villagers scattered quickly. The Buddha's love for the elephant gradually soothed the elephant's mind. The beast slowed down and grew calm. The elephant stopped in front of the Buddha and sank down onto his knees. The Buddha stroked the elephant's head. Calm had been restored.

Background: begin as 5. Add claves for scattering villagers. Gradually slow everything down and fade out, leaving the background tune to slow down to a calm peaceful slow speed as at the beginning.

Music Attainment Target: 1
Main Focus: Composing
Key Stage: 2

English Attainment Target: 1 & 2
Main Focus: Hindu Story

Situations

Suggested Materials

Cards with 'situations' (see example). Percussion.

1. Situations are displayed for all the class to see. The teacher discusses with the children the characteristics of each situation, encouraging the children to think of how these might be represented in sound, e.g.

   – Headteacher telling child off
   – Nurse talking to a patient
   – Two motorists arguing
   – Father looking after baby
   – Two old people chattering
   – Two people at a football match

2. The children get into pairs and choose a situation. They select appropriate instruments and rehearse a sequence.

3. They perform their 'conversation' to the other children. Can the audience identify which situation is being represented?

Extension Activities

1. Extend the activity to role-play drama activities. Children may like to use some of their sounds to accompany the dramatic pieces. The children may also come up with their own 'Situations'.

2. Can the children find ways of recording their sequences? Encourage them to consider how they might record elements such as dynamics, pitch, rhythm, etc.

Music Attainment Target: 1 & 2	English Attainment Target: 1
Main Focus: Composing	Main Focus: Role-play
Key Stage: 2	

Appendix

Glossary

Crescendo — Getting louder.

Decrescendo — Getting quieter.

Drone — One or more notes maintained throughout a piece.

Dynamics — The gradations of volume in music.

Form — The order in which different ideas appear in a piece of music.

Improvisation — Composing spontaneously while performing.

Glissando — The process of moving from one note to another quickly, while playing all other notes in between.

Notation — The symbolic written representation of sound(s).

Ostinato — A rhythm or melody pattern repeated regularly during a piece of music (often as accompaniment).

Pitch — The perception of sounds as 'high' or 'low' in relation to each other. A woman's voice is usually higher in pitch than a man's.

Pulse — A repetitive, regular beat (sometimes silent), which can indicate the speed of a piece of music.

Rest — 'Musical silence' – the absence of a sounding note or notes.

Rhythm — The pattern which long and short sounds and rests make when heard in sequence.

Rhythmic independence — The ability to maintain a rhythm against other rhythms.

Score — A written record of all the parts in a piece of music.

Sequencing — The ordering of sounds.

Timbre — The characteristics/colour of sound(s).

Volume — The loudness or quietness of sound/music.

Symbols

f — Loud

p — Quiet

< — Getting louder

> — Getting quieter

Pentatonic Scales

The notes on tuned percussion should be arranged with long bars to the left, getting increasingly smaller to the right-hand side, and in alphabetical order. Most (but not all) start with 'C'.

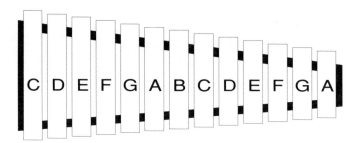

By removing any note 'B' and any note 'F', it is possible to have a five-note scale, called 'Pentatonic' (Penta = five). This should leave a sequence of C D E G A.

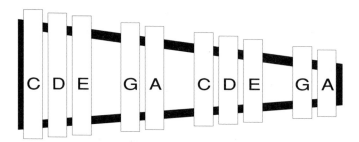

A pentatonic scale is useful for improvising melodies, both solo and in group work.

Occasionally instruments will come with notes called 'sharps' (with a ♯ after the letter), and 'flats' (with a ♭ after the letter), e.g. C♯ E♭ F♯ G♯ B♭. By using only these notes, it is again possible to create a pentatonic scale. This same scale can be found by just using the black notes on a piano or keyboard. Use this scale if most of the notes on your tuned percussion are sharps and flats.